A *Little Guide* FOR
OFFICE SANITY

T0364057

RP Minis®
Hachette Book Group
1290 Avenue of the Americas, New York, NY 10104
www.runningpress.com
@Running_Press

First Edition: September 2021

Published by RP Minis, an imprint of Perseus Books, LLC, a subsidiary of Hachette Book Group, Inc. The RP Minis name and logo is a registered trademark of the Hachette Book Group.

The publisher is not responsible for websites (or their content) that are not owned by the publisher.

ISBN: 978-0-7624-7375-5

CONTENTS

INTRODUCTION

Water-cooler talk is one of the best things about the office. When you're not quite ready to dive into your work, it's a real asset to be able to kill time having conversations like this one:

YOU: "Morning, Joe! How was the weekend?"

JOE: "Oh, good! We took the kids for a hike, and Carol and I started the new season of *The Great British Bake Off.*"

YOU: "Ooh, no spoilers! I haven't watched it yet!"

What a treat! But sometimes you have days that are *so* busy. And Joe is no longer the friendly guy you want to share a casual kitchen-nook conversation with; he's the guy who won't. Stop. Asking. You. For. Stuff. And Joe is not the only one. Some days it seems like it's just one inter-ruption after the next.

Don't worry. There are solutions. *The Little Guide for Office Sanity* will help you navigate every kind of distraction that might come along during your workday, and it comes with a handy number-ticket dispenser for those who just don't quite . . . *get the message*.

Take a number, Joe! I'll be with you in a while!

There are many different types of distractions that you may encounter during your day, but the two most often cited? People and technology. The following tips and tricks will help you navigate how to politely and professionally rid yourself of these nuisances and bring a little sanity back into your day.

PEOPLE PROBLEMS

Picture this: it's 11:15 a.m., you've got 45 minutes to finish the very-urgent project you're working on, and who comes a-knockin'? Joe. He's looking for help with his Outlook. Since when are you IT? Did you try turning your computer off and turning it back on, Joe?

But it's not just Joe. At the exact moment that Joe is leaning in with his computer, your phone rings. It's Barb—asking if you've submitted that expense report yet. And then Gary stops by real casual-like, wondering if it was *today* you two were meeting, or *tomorrow*? And Lucy—sweet Lucy!—popping over to see how exactly you wanted her to format the volunteer sign-up list (in list format, Lucy).

PEOPLE PROBLEMS
Solution #1:

TAKE A NUMBER

So many people bothering you, so little time (literally). The solution? Tell them to take a number! With this number-ticket dispenser, everyone can take their very own personal number and keep an eye (from afar!) on your desk to see when their number comes up. Soon you won't even have to say anything. When someone stops by, just smile and point at the ticket dispenser. They'll know what to do.

PEOPLE PROBLEMS
Solution #2:

CUE THE HEADPHONES

Another way to quickly tell people *now's not the time*? Headphones. You put those headphones on—the bigger and more expensive-looking, the better—and it's like an invisible force field around you. A big sign that says, *I'm very focused and very busy, don't you dare distract me.* You're sitting there enjoying your music or your favorite podcast (or maybe nothing at all—your secret's safe with us) and suddenly you're interruption-proof. And if someone does have the gall to stop by and say your name, you'll just want to perfect that straight-faced-staring-ahead look, like you have no idea in the world someone is saying your name. How could you be expected to hear them? You've got *head-phones on*.

PEOPLE PROBLEMS
Solution #3:

FAKE MEETINGS FOR REAL SUCCESS

Warning: This is only for *professional distraction escapers*, not to be tried by newbies. After years of avoiding interruptions, you may be ready for the big kahuna: a fake meeting. "Oh, sorry Kevin! I'd *love* to hear more about your kid's soccer game, but I've got to run to a meeting!" Obviously you'll want to have a go-to meeting topic and room number/name on hand for the extra nosy. And you'll want to have a place you can go to hide out until Kevin is out of sight. If Kevin catches you back at your desk too soon, just remember: fake meetings can have fake cancellations, too.

TECH TEMPTATIONS

Those of us who work in an office can agree: technology advancements are mostly a good thing. For example, there aren't too many of us that have to save paper receipts anymore—we can just snap a photo. Most printouts have gone digital. And gone are the days of fax machines and their frustrating sounds and lights and tendency to eat up paper that leave you confused and wondering, *So . . . are we good here?* But some newfangled technology can be incredibly distracting.

The following three scenarios and super-simple solutions will help you avoid those tempting technology moments. Soon they'll be a thing of the past, just like fax machines.

TECH TEMPTATION
Solution #1:

PUT THAT PHONE AWAY

We all know how fun group texts can be, how they can turn a boring day into a laugh-out-loud good time. But between texting, social media, checking your messages and comments and likes—it can be extremely distracting. Suddenly it's lunchtime and you've hardly touched anything even remotely resembling work.

We've got good news—this one is extremely easy to fix: leave your phone at home. We promise, it will be okay! *You* will be okay. It sounds scary, but it's really not. You'll be amazed at how good you feel not checking your phone every two minutes and how much you get done.

Fine, fine, fine, if that's really too terrifying for you, bring your phone to work, but leave it in your desk drawer! One super fun thing about this solution? When you finally do look at your phone again, you'll have about 74 text messages from those group texts to catch up on—at *home*!

TECH TEMPTATION
Solution #2:

"BROKEN" PHONE

As little kids, we all imagined our-selves at our future desks, right? We were wearing super-*professional* outfits in these daydreams, and we're answering the phone all the time: "Hello, Sally speaking." But in reality, answering the phone at work is just another way to eat up time. People get chatty on the phone, they want to *talk*. This just won't do.

There is a super-easy solution: unplug it. If anyone asks, just give a good eye roll, flash an *I'm so inconvenienced* face, and say something like "Yeah, I reached out to IT about it but I haven't heard back." Shake your fist at the air to really sell it. "Curse you, IT!!!"

TECH
TEMPTATION
Solution #3:

LET IT GO

Sometimes good intentions can lead to bad distractions. Ever heard of Inbox Zero? It's the idea that you keep your inbox completely free of emails. Every email that comes in, you take care of it and file it away. Keeping your inbox low really is a good idea so you don't have to comb through hundreds (or for some people, thousands) of emails every time you want to find something. However, becoming obsessed with the idea can lead to answering and handling every single email as soon as it comes in. No matter what you're doing, even if you're chugging along on a project, you stop, read the email, and quick! Change paths!

Suddenly you're fielding questions, searching for something on the server, answering emails all day— and not tackling anything on your own to-do list.

Super-simple solution number three: close your inbox. Just for a half-hour, an hour maybe—enough time to get some work done. This will feel scary at first—you'll wonder *What am I missing? How many emails are piling up?* But the more you do this, the more you'll realize that rarely does an emergency come up in the 30 minutes you're not looking at your email.

And another pro tip? Schedule time on your calendar each week for email clean-up—it will be like a *productive* distraction when you need a break from all that work you're actually getting done.

FLIP THE SCRIPT:
Distractions as Rewards

We paint distractions as kind of evil in this little guide, but that's not entirely true. You can also use "distractions" as motivation! For example, maybe after spending forty-five minutes on an important project, you reward yourself with five minutes to zone out, meditate, stare out the window. Or when

you're having trouble wrapping something up, tell yourself that as soon as you finish it, you can go down and get a treat from the vending machine or enjoy one of the donuts that Joe brought in— and maybe you can even pick up your conversation about *The Great British Bake Off* with him. You'll be surprised how much more productive you can be when you have a reward waiting for you.

IN CONCLUSION

We get it! Distractions are all over the place. Sneaky little ninjas always out to get you! But with these tips and tricks, you just might be able to get some work done. You can thank us later—after you finish that thing you *really* need to get done today.

This book has been bound using handcraft methods and Smyth-sewn to ensure durability.

Illustrated by Sean Tulgetske.
Designed by Celeste Joyce.
Written by Mollie Thomas.